WEDDING MUSIC
FOR CLASSICAL PLAYERS

To access companion recorded piano accompaniments online, visit:
www.halleonard.com/mylibrary

Enter Code
1422-2197-3573-3815

ISBN: 978-1-5400-2040-6

HAL•LEONARD®

Visit Hal Leonard Online at
www.halleonard.com

Contact Us:
Hal Leonard
7777 West Bluemound Road
Milwaukee, WI 53213
Email: info@halleonard.com

In Europe contact:
Hal Leonard Europe Limited
42 Wigmore Street
Marylebone, London, W1U 2RN
Email: info@halleonardeurope.com

In Australia contact:
Hal Leonard Australia Pty. Ltd.
4 Lentara Court
Cheltenham, Victoria, 3192 Australia
Email: info@halleonard.com.au

Depending on the situation, sometimes wedding service music must be abbreviated or expanded. Feel free to find optional cuts, endings, or repeated sections as needed.

CONTENTS

Pianists on the recordings: [1]Brendan Fox, [2]Judit Jaimes, [3]Richard Walters

The price of this publication includes access to companion recorded piano accompaniments online,
for download or streaming, using the unique code found on the title page.

Visit **www.halleonard.com/mylibrary** and enter the access code.

Air
from Orchestral Suite No. 3 in D Major, BWV 1068

Johann Sebastian Bach
Transcribed by Celeste Avery

Arioso
(Sinfonia)
from Cantata, BWV 156

Johann Sebastian Bach
Transcribed by Celeste Avery

Jesu, joy of man's desiring
from Cantata, BWV 147

Johann Sebastian Bach
Transcribed by Celeste Avery

* fermata for optional ending only

Minuet
from String Quintet in E Major, Op. 11, No. 5

Luigi Boccherini
Transcribed by Celeste Avery

Ave Maria

adapted from Prelude in C Major, BWV 846 by Johann Sebastian Bach

Charles Gounod
Transcribed by Celeste Avery

Hornpipe
from *Water Music*, HWV 348

George Frideric Handel
Transcribed by Celeste Avery

La Réjouissance

from *Music for the Royal Fireworks*, HWV 351

George Frideric Handel
Transcribed by Celeste Avery

Largo

(Ombra mai fù)

from *Serse*, HWV 40

George Frideric Handel
Transcribed by Celeste Avery

Jupiter Chorale
from *The Planets*

Gustav Holst
Transcribed by Celeste Avery

WEDDING MUSIC
FOR CLASSICAL PLAYERS

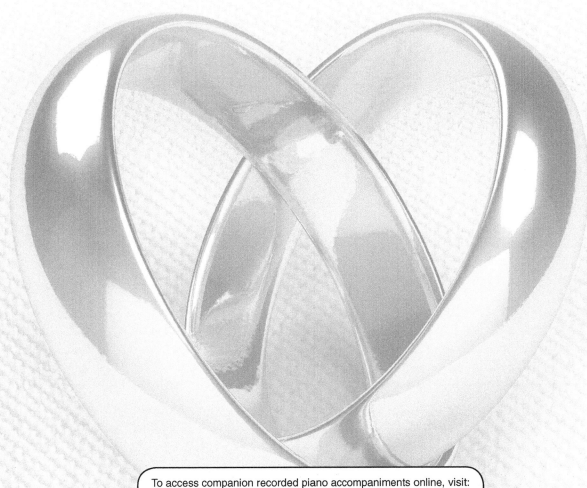

To access companion recorded piano accompaniments online, visit:
www.halleonard.com/mylibrary

Enter Code
7756-8343-3621-0683

ISBN: 978-1-5400-2040-6

Visit Hal Leonard Online at
www.halleonard.com

Contact Us:
Hal Leonard
7777 West Bluemound Road
Milwaukee, WI 53213
Email: info@halleonard.com

In Europe contact:
Hal Leonard Europe Limited
42 Wigmore Street
Marylebone, London, W1U 2RN
Email: info@halleonardeurope.com

In Australia contact:
Hal Leonard Australia Pty. Ltd.
4 Lentara Court
Cheltenham, Victoria, 3192 Australia
Email: info@halleonard.com.au

Depending on the situation, sometimes wedding service music must be abbreviated or expanded. Feel free to find optional cuts, endings, or repeated sections as needed.

CONTENTS

Pianists on the recordings: [1]Brendan Fox, [2]Judit Jaimes, [3]Richard Walters

The price of this publication includes access to companion recorded piano accompaniments online,

for download or streaming, using the unique code found on the title page.

Visit **www.halleonard.com/mylibrary** and enter the access code.

Air

from Orchestral Suite No. 3 in D Major, BWV 1068

Johann Sebastian Bach
Transcribed by Celeste Avery

* This repeat is omitted on the companion accompaniment recording.

The pianist plays the following as an introduction on the companion accompaniment recording:

Arioso
(Sinfonia)
from Cantata, BWV 156

Johann Sebastian Bach
Transcribed by Celeste Avery

The pianist plays the following as an introduction on the companion accompaniment recording:

Jesu, joy of man's desiring

from Cantata, BWV 147

Johann Sebastian Bach
Transcribed by Celeste Avery

*optional ending

poco rit.   a tempo

rit.

* fermata for optional ending only

Minuet
from String Quintet in E Major, Op. 11, No. 5

Luigi Boccherini
Transcribed by Celeste Avery

The pianist plays the following as an introduction on the companion accompaniment recording:

* This repeat is omitted on the companion accompaniment recording.

Hornpipe

from *Water Music*, HWV 348

George Frideric Handel
Transcribed by Celeste Avery

* This repeat is omitted on the companion accompaniment recording.

* This repeat is omitted on the companion accompaniment recording.

Ave Maria
adapted from Prelude in C Major, BWV 846 by Johann Sebastian Bach

Charles Gounod
Transcribed by Celeste Avery

La Réjouissance

from *Music for the Royal Fireworks*, HWV 351

George Frideric Handel
Transcribed by Celeste Avery

The pianist plays the following as an introduction on the companion accompaniment recording:

Largo

(Ombra mai fù)

from *Serse*, HWV 40

George Frideric Handel
Transcribed by Celeste Avery

Jupiter Chorale
from *The Planets*

Gustav Holst
Transcribed by Celeste Avery

The pianist plays the following as an introduction on the companion accompaniment recording:

Meditation
from *Thaïs*

Jules Massenet

* For a shorter version, begin here after two measures of introduction.

Wedding March

from *A Midsummer Night's Dream*, Op. 61

Felix Mendelssohn
Transcribed by Celeste Avery

Canon in D

Johann Pachelbel
Transcribed by Celeste Avery

Gymnopédie No. 1

from *Trois Gymnopédies*

Erik Satie
Transcribed by Celeste Avery

For a shorter performance, the piece may begin at measure 40.

Ave Maria

Franz Schubert
Transcribed by Celeste Avery

Bist du bei mir
(You Are with Me)

Gottfried Heinrich Stölzel
Transcribed by Celeste Avery

Bridal Chorus
from *Lohengrin*

Richard Wagner
Transcribed by Celeste Avery

* For a shorter version, begin here after four measures of introduction.

Meditation
from *Thaïs*

Jules Massenet

* For a shorter version, begin here after two measures of introduction.

Wedding March

from *A Midsummer Night's Dream*, Op. 61

Felix Mendelssohn
Transcribed by Celeste Avery

Bridal Chorus
from *Lohengrin*

Richard Wagner
Transcribed by Celeste Avery

* For a shorter version, begin here after four measures of introduction.

Canon in D

Johann Pachelbel
Transcribed by Celeste Avery

Gymnopédie No. 1

from *Trois Gymnopédies*

Erik Satie
Transcribed by Celeste Avery

For a shorter performance, the piece may begin at measure 40.

Ave Maria

Franz Schubert
Transcribed by Celeste Avery

Bist du bei mir
(You Are with Me)

Gottfried Heinrich Stölzel
Transcribed by Celeste Avery